Intolerable Ferocity

THE PAST	5
07.01.2003	27
15.01.2003	46
22.01.2003	73
THE FRIENDSHIP STARTS	91
30.01.2003	100
LATER ON:	119
07.02.2003	130
14.02.2003	148

The first time

The past

As far back as I can remember, I've never had it easy, growing with a drunk as a father and a mother that couldn't focus on me because she was busy babysitting the drunk. I grew up thinking that all men were pigs, that act like children when they are intoxicated. I remember my dad being hauled into bed by the five of us (my younger brother and sister, my older sister and me, and my mother) after he had one too many. Sometimes we would have to pick him up from the tavern drunk as a skunk. It would be so shameful as we could barely lift him. People would smirk and judge us as we pulled and pushed him into our car.

I guess from an early age; this is what I was exposed to growing up. When I was a child, I would have to tiptoe into the room where my father slept because the rules were simple; if we woke him up, we would sleep beside him, missing school. Not to mention the abuse that followed; he liked to cuddle us and not in an excellent way.

My mother being dragged by this horrible individual, acting like her husband, my so-called father. I remember him forcing her to do whatever he wanted her to do. We would stand outside their bedroom door and hear as things broke and clothes were torn. And soon after, we would listen to the sounds of moans and groans by our mother as the bed creaked heavily. I remember he would scream and shout as a thumping and clapping sound would occur soon after, and more things broke and the glass shattered. She never told us what happened during the night hours in their bedroom.

It got so bad that the police were called on occasion by the neighbours as things broke in the house regularly and not to mention our head being used as a ball to break them. Of course, my mother never pressed charges, as she always said, "what would people say and think."

Of course, soon as the police would leave, my father would come out with his old routine of apologies, which would last for a couple of months as he "gave up alcohol" supposedly.

Then sooner or later, it would start again. But it was nice to have some normality of beautiful family life, even if it was only for a few months.

I never understood why my father abused a defenseless woman.

Why would a man beat a woman and then apologize to do it all over again?

If you know it's wrong, why do it?

I have forgotten the number of times I have picked up broken ornaments off the floor with blood on them.

The number of times we have heeled from cuts and bruises, I remember everyone.

I have been scarred for life, and I can never trust any man in the future because of my past.

They all act nice when they want something. Soon as they have what they want, then we become a tool rather than a person.

No more will I put up with any man.

In the future, in my life, men will either be controlled or manipulated as my father used to do to us.

Because somebody has to pay the price, it's not fair what happened to us. I see all these nice families, and they seem to have everything.

In terms of a loving father figure in their life

Why didn't we have this? I'm so jealous.

Men are not the boss of me; when I get a man in my life, he will worship the ground I walk on. I promise you that.

Or I will hurt him and take all my anger out on him; I can't live with men and can't live without them in this male-dominated era.

I guess that's why I am the way I am; I don't care for worldly things as everything I liked growing up, my father either broke or threw away.

From this, I became a strong, resilient woman. I want a man to get out of order with me so I can put him in his place like my mother could never do.

I learned essential and valuable lessons as I grew up. Each time I was beaten, I saw ways to manipulate certain situations and play upon things.

Perhaps this is why I like to ruin things when people do nice things for me. I am not used to niceties because of what he did to us.

Because I saw and learned how my father would get around my mother when I needed to, he would use her vulnerability to aid in his comfort.

My mother came from a well-respected family and had backward postmodern views on women and how they should behave in marriage. So, my father would threaten divorce each time he wanted my mother to comply with any requests. My mother would be fearful of her father, finding out that she hadn't been a 'proper wife.' So, she begged my father not to inform her dad, and in return, she would be taken advantage of in the worst possible ways.

From this, I learned how to bend men to my will; I saw how my father twisted words to comply with his life method. He acted like he was the injured one after abusing my mother for nearly a lifetime.

I remember my mother running out of the house to seek comfort at the neighbour's house because sometimes it just got that bad. But my father would calm down and bring my mother home, explaining to the neighbour that her hysterical outbursts were an illness or mental disorder and nothing else.

And further, lie stating she was off her medication. Apologize to the neighbour and then give my mother the same sob story that he will quit drinking and turn a new page in his life. Of course, it was all a lie, but each time my father reset himself, we all knew of the next few months of peace that was headed our way.

It was like the storm had passed, and now we could all heal and mend our broken dreams and hopes of a better tomorrow.

I remembered the day when my brother grew up into a man sooner than expected. That day, my brother stopped the abuse from reoccurring as he grew more substantial than my father and was able to maltreat him into submission.

That day I knew how I was going to tame my man in the future. But I wasn't going to use force; after all, how could I? I was just a young defenseless woman.

SO,

I started to compile ways to manipulate my future man into submission by finding out all his secrets and then using them against him when I saw fit because all men are horrible to faced liars who need a woman to guide them along their path.

Because I saw how venerable men are when they are drunk. Question a man while drunk and find the answer you are looking for.

My mother stood behind my father, holding him up through thick and thin. She single-handedly bought up four kids, worked 12 hours a day at home. They say, "there is a strong woman behind everyman." I say, "there is a helpless man in front of a strong woman."

The woman's time has arrived, and in the future, the men in my life will mistake love for obedience; and compassion for manipulation. My passion will be to make sure my past does not dictate my future. But it will because the dictator will be a scorned woman. Who has father issues of the worst kind, so all you men watch out, I'm not your 'babe to be taken advantage of'?

I remember, I dated this guy, he was devoted to me, I would go as far to say he was 'head over heels for me' I mean that's all that was missing after I took his balls.

Do you get what I mean? He fell in love with me, and I just ripped out his heart and laughed in his face.

Because I could see he was only going to use me for sex. I would let him touch me until I came, then walk away, leaving him begging for more and more.

Until one day, he imploded. He claimed that I was not serving his needs; I knew what that meant straight away, 'control.'

I told him not to be a douche bag, find a prostitute or an easy woman or a man if that's your fancy, to satisfy his urges. Why should I have sex with somebody with who I don't feel like doing it?

After all, I can still hear my mother asking my father to stop. And my father taking 'no' as a 'yes' and carrying on.

I could see right through these guys claiming to like me; I mean, they were straight out of a comic book.

I mean, they all come to look at my features and then lean into a conversation that was stating the obvious, always.

It was like meeting Joey Tribiani from Friends every time I met a guy.

They all well like a cliché, using the famous 'how you are doing' phrase from Friends. Of course, they never got it right, and all I would see is want to be Joey. So, as they wanted to be a joey, I treated them as one.

I was a beautiful young woman ready to meet the guy I could treat ferociously, and more importantly, he would be compliant to my intolerable ferocity. I needed an uneducated person, who perhaps couldn't see me undermining him.

Although I meet some dashing men, I could see they have had the same ideas in mind. I needed a man's man. Who could be compelled to meet my demands and wishes? Yes, I needed a slave, someone who did what they were told!

Just as my mother controls my dad nowadays through the fear of my brother

So, I waited until someone prevailed into my life; some people say that "you find what you're looking for when you're not looking for it."

I know it's a cliché, but this is what happened to me. I was surprised at how I met this guy that made me fall in love with him. I mean, it takes a lot for me to drop my defenses, but this guy was different.

I suppose in many ways; he was one of those black sheep, those people that never really fit into society.

Looking at him, I realize that I had found what I was looking for. He seemed vulnerable but yet jack the lad. He looks healthy but seems to struggle with emotion. He seemed to like his alcohol, so for me, it will be easier to control him. Not to mention he's outstanding looking, so at least I can let him ravish me to my end.

Hahaha,

I wonder if he's got a big one. I guess we will have to see how hard the headboard moves, lol (laughing out loud).

I'm so horny. After all, women need it just as much as men. I want to use this guy for intimacy and perhaps to carry my bags home. Well, I might as well get some fun out of it. Just in case he doesn't have a big one—Lmao (Laughing my ass off).

He could make me laugh, though, because each time I saw him, he made me wet. It was like I pissed myself. Seriously my knickers would need changing throughout the day. I can only imagine what it is like when he pushes his gearstick up my shaft.

I don't know; with this guy, it seems to be all about the sex.

Anyway, this is how I met him.

So, this is what happened:

07.01.2003

The bus number 22

I was coming home on the bus from college, the same bus that I caught every day. With the same old idiots that tried to get in my knickers. It just got harder and harder to ignore their advances but
I pull out my book and ignore the advances from anybody because they were not worth my time.

I remember distinctly my concentration was momentarily broken by this loud person that had got on the bus. He was intoxicated, and his words were slurped. I remember he could barely stand, but yet he seems to balance himself well. He seems to enjoy himself and talk to strangers effortlessly.

I don't know what it was, but I was fascinated with him; I could see him coming towards me, so I ducked down into my book, pretending to read it, but really, I was intrigued by this drunken fool. Each time he spoke, a smile came about me. I tried to hide the smile behind the book. But I couldn't help myself.

For the moment, he had my attention.

It is not the sort of guy that I usually am into, but he was funny. I remember when he sat down opposite me. He never once looked at my features. Although he tried to start conversations with me, he never said anything out of place.

I pretended to be shy, I acknowledged him, but I didn't say a word. I remember thinking I could control him; for some odd reason, he started talking, and as he rambled on, he said the words that I was dying to hear from any man.

"He said he didn't mind a woman controlling him." Of course, he wasn't speaking to me; I think you talked to the entire bus; I kept smiling, ducking down behind my book until he realized that I was interested. He said, you have a beautiful smile; I got to thinking, can you see my smile through the book. Of course, the book was not covering my smile all the time.

I felt embarrassed but turned on also. The waterworks downstairs seems to drip a tad or two.

I replied forcibly with a polite yet abrupt 'hello.'

Add this point; he started to focus only on me.

He started talking and rambling on about everything and anything.

This guy could talk to save the world; I remember thinking.

But I could see that he was lonely and sad inside. Because each time he stopped talking, he had a frown on his face. This was a guy covering up his hurt through alcohol.

I don't know why; for some reason, I wanted this guy. I wanted him to embrace me, hold me, and be with me.

In that moment of madness, this guy inadvertently took hold of me.

I think that day, something inside changed in me.

I could see that not all men were egotistically and emotionally deranged.

I mean, this guy didn't even have pride. He was just hysterically stupid, but looking at his big bulging arms, I could see straight away that he was a man's man. So, some of my boxes got ticked.

I tried to look away because I didn't want to be with a drunk. But I didn't know what it was; perhaps I used to drunken men. I don't know. I mean, my father was a drunk, and my brother followed suit behind. So maybe my future man, perhaps a drunk too?

So, as I sat there on the bus, my ideal man was supposedly sitting in front of me.

Could this be, I wondered. I looked at him repeatedly as a bit off my lip.

For some reason or another, I just wanted to touch his bulging biceps.

But for some reason, my eyes kept losing altitude from his biceps to his manhood.

I couldn't help myself.

I wanted to squeeze his manhood;

I mean his biceps. Lol.

But his manhood kept getting in the way. lol

I bet he has a big one.

Oh my God, what's wrong with me, as I spoke to myself.

Was I gagging for it? I don't know. I guess this is what they mean when they say, "sexually frustrated women are dangerous."

Well, in my defense, I was still a virgin. And I was waiting for somebody to plow me.

So, many thoughts were going through my head. I never thought it possible. But this guy was bringing this side of me out.

I guess I was coming out of the closet. Well, at least out of the doll's house. Lol.

He seemed a free spirit, because although everybody else was quietly seated on the bus. This bumbling idiot saw too enjoy awkwardly lavishly talking about anything to anyone who would pay attention to him.

He was a proper drunken gentleman; I mean, based on what my father used to do while he was intoxicated, this guy seems to do the opposite.

I wanted him to ask me out; I wanted so desperately to say yes.

But this guy kept evading asking me out; he instead focused on what we would do as a couple if we were dating rather than start the ball rolling.

My inner child was screaming at him to ask me out.

Each time the bus would stop, my heart would skip a beat because I would know on one of these stops, one of us will get off.

I mean, what are the chances of us living in the same postcode.

I think he was scared that I would say no, as he gazed into my eyes, looking at nothing else other than touching my soul with his energy.

The more he looked into my eyes, the more I nearly leaned in. But I had to force myself not to make the first move.

I remember I looked away for a second, and all of a sudden, I saw an empty seat. I looked about to see that he had walked towards the other end of the bus because his stopped had arrived.

I felt so disappointed; I wanted to get up and shout:

"What's your number, your gorgeous hunk."

Something magical happened, something entirely unexpected, but yet somehow it did happen.

As I put my book up to duck behind it once more, that guy

spoke loudly, getting hold of my attention once more.

He said,

"Excuse me, excuse me miss, but I like you, and I was wondering if you would like to date me."

I didn't know what to say, so I just ducked behind my book.

A lady leaned over from beside me and said, "excuse me, I think he's talking to you."

I looked at him once more, he smiled, and he said,

"Call me; my number is in your book."

How he managed to put his number in my book is still a mystery today. But I must admit it was heart-warming to know that I had his contact details.

Has he got ready to get off the bus, he rudely and loudly said?

"I like that girl in the corner of the bus which has taken my heart today."

The bus stopped, and he got off; the lady next to me said, "well, aren't you the lucky one."

I was embarrassed, but I was excited that I had his number.

Somehow at some point, this person managed to put his business card in between my legs.

I mean my pages,

OMG (oh my God), what's wrong with me as I spoke to myself in my thoughts. As I ducked behind my book once more, rolling my eyes at everybody.

How he managed to place his business card between my PAGES, this will always dupe me;

was he a magician; must've been a magician of some sort.

After that day, I wanted to ring him, but I promised myself I would never go out with a drunk.

I didn't want to be associated with alcohol, but there was just something about this guy.

Was I destined to be around alcoholics all my life? I don't know. It just felt right in my heart. Not to mention, he did say, "I could control him."

I was intrigued.

I couldn't shake it; I just wanted to talk to him. But at the same time, my morals prohibited me from ringing him.

I couldn't go out with somebody who resembled my dad or my brother.

That was the end of the story!

So, I thought,

15.01.2003

The bar

Nearly a week past and I couldn't get this guy out of my mind.

Each time I thought about him, a warm smile became me.

I wanted to talk to him; there's something about him, but I could not put my finger on it.

Perhaps if we met each other again; maybe just for a coffee,

Oh, I don't know.

Could I stretch my morals, to perhaps a coffee? And maybe ease that tingly feeling down below.

After all, not knowing the answers to my questions was starting to stress me out somewhat.

Perhaps I could get him to stop drinking.

Perhaps I could control him to stop drinking.

Perhaps I could get him to be a man that I liked.

But I like him the way he is. That was the problem.

So, for that reason, I to listen to my morals; I remember my father and what you did to my mother, I wasn't going to risk that.

So, I didn't call him.

I just pretended he was just like my father and moved past it.

I went shopping with my friend; I knew for most of my adult life to take my mind off him.

We went into all the shops we usually go into and did what we usually did.

Which was to try on all the clothes that we wanted and buy none of them

We just took pictures of each other wearing different clothes.

This is one way some women tend to have so many pictures of themselves on social media with different clothes on.

As we were trying on some close, my tap started trickling again. I don't think my friend saw it.

But I remember walking out of the store with knickers that I didn't pay for because I was so embarrassed by what had happened in the changing rooms.

For some reason, I kept smiling; I think I was thinking about him.

My friend and I later went for some drinks.

And before you think otherwise.

It was soft drinks.

I remember I kept daydreaming about him. And each time, I smile would find itself on my face.

My friend could see my sneaky smile,

She asked me

"Who is he then."

I replied, "whatever do you mean."

She said, 'you have the kind of smile of a woman who has met her man."

I replied, "you don't know what you're talking about."

She said, "whatever, you will eventually tell me anyway."

She also said, (come on, spill the beans).

I replied, "some guy gave me his phone number on the bus coming home last week."

She said, "on the bus, did you call him? I hope you didn't, because you meet all sorts of weirdos on the bus.

I replied, "yeah, he was a bit weird."

She said, "but he's making you smile, did anything happens."

I replied, "whatever do you mean."

She said, "you know what I mean" she looked deeply into my eyes and said, "you like this one, don't you; don't reply; I can tell."

I replied, "I don't think I'm going to see him again."

She said, "there's a difference between not seeing him again and you want to see him again."

I replied as I clenched my arms together and dropped my head towards the ground and said, "I wouldn't mind."

So anyway,

After a lengthy discussion with my friend, we realized that I didn't want to be with a drunk.

So, I tore up the piece of paper with his number on it in front of my friend and left it at that.

I guess I left it up to fate.

It's either that

or

Is his business card in my back-pocket still, hmm I wonder; and did I tear up just a piece of paper hmm?

Well, mums the word, shhh. I won't tell f you won't, dear reader.

After all, I didn't want to leave everything to chance.

I wanted to make a point in front of my friend. As you do!!!

But anyway, I don't think I will call him.

But I do want to call him.

There was something about him unless I just fancy drunken guys.

Anyway,

Time flies when you are shopping, so as it was getting a bit late, my friend and I started walking out the door and down the street to catch the bus home.

My friend and I had quite a lengthy conversation over several tropical juice drinks.

And as we were heading towards the bus stop, she needed to pee.

So, I saw this lovely bar and decided that I would ask if she could use their ladies' room.

So, my friend and I went into this bar and asked the barkeep if we could use the lady's restroom.

I remember thinking that this person behind the bar is a right douche bag because, just like every other man, he eyed us up and down while taking visual pictures of our features. Some men are such perverts.

However, the pervert barkeep said that we could use the restroom if we bought a drink because only the bathrooms were for customers. So, I bought a drink, another orange juice, as my friend went to the restroom.

I remember having the same feeling at the bar as I did on the bus. I couldn't figure out why I wasn't talking to anybody, but I could feel some energy.

And for some reason or another, I just wanted to smile, but then that would have sent the wrong signal to the pervert barkeep.

So, I stood there and took a sip out of my orange juice. The guy next to me turned around, and to my surprise, it was the same guy from the bus.

He had to look twice because I think he thought his luck came in.

I didn't know what to do, as I was happily shocked and surprised. As he turned around and said, "oh hello, I know you, you're the girl from the bus."

So, I did the one thing I could. I ran out of the bar with my friend following me shortly behind. We quickly ran out into this alleyway and hid.

My friend asking me, "what happened," I just said to her, "be quiet" I was excited and scared at the same time.

I saw him come out of the bar, I saw him look left and right, and I just wanted to run up behind him and hold him tight and never let him go.

But he was in a bar, and probably getting drunk, which put a dent into what I was thinking.

If nothing else, I wanted to date him to talk to him and maybe hold his hand.

What's wrong with me, is this love so, I said to my friend.

My friend just giggled and said:

 "This is something you need to work on and figure out for yourself."

"Come on; we are going to miss the bus."

"But yes, I do think you like this one a tad more than the rest."

As we ran towards the bus

I couldn't stop thinking about him at this point because this is the second time we met.

I just kept thinking, what if I rang him. I knew I should've given him my telephone number.

That way, all the power would've been in my hands to say yes or no.

If I ring him now, it's going to look like that I want him.

Why does he have to be so complicated?

Maybe I should call him and have a one-night stand. At least that way, the tingle down below will stop tingling. And perhaps I can get the waterworks under control too.

Fucking hell, I'm so horny.

Oh my God, what am I thinking; they say that the woman knows in the first instance if she wants to be with the man sexually.

But I think it's after the first kiss, so why do I feel like I want to rip his shirt off and kisses body all over.

Fucking hell, I didn't just say that!

This is unlike me; I am a proper lady. Yet I want to scream out the words "fucking."

I'll tell you one thing for sure, if I meet him again entirely by chance, I will agree to date him once.

Or perhaps have a phone conversation with him, maybe a dirty phone conversation with him.

Oh, stop it, you, silly cow.

As I talk to myself,

I have started talking to myself recently.

I can't help myself thinking dirty thoughts about him.

I mean, I haven't been with many men, well, to be honest, I've only ever let one boyfriend touch me with his hands.

I was a young woman that hadn't had sexual intercourse just yet.

I wanted to wait until I got married, but this guy makes me wet.

At first, I thought it was a discharge because I've never really focused on things happening down there.

I know when it's that time of the month, but I don't know what happens under the sheets.

Call me naïve, but I didn't care for that sort of thing. Until now, that is.

So, these were the kind of thoughts that I was having.

And I didn't know why; I guess I knew why; I didn't know how to express myself to others in that manner.

But I did need to do something soon because I'm using like three pairs of knickers a day.

Is this what sex feels like. I mean, sometimes I want to discharge all over his face.

I get these wild urges from time to time, and I don't know what to do with it other than write it all in my diary.

I can imagine them pressed up against his muscular chest and him holding me tight within his grasp with his bulging arms.

I wish he would tear my clothes off and have me and be done with it. I think I need to come; maybe come on his face.

Oh, my days, what's wrong with me?

Is this what is sexually frustrated feels like?

Or am I just gagging for it?

Sometimes my mind wanders, but I guess I am a woman, and I'm allowed to have these kinds of thoughts.

I mean, it's got so bad lately that I look forward to my period.

Because for some reason, when I'm on, I'm also switched off from these constant thoughts.

So anyway, I'm going to leave it to fate,

I know I said this before, but in my defense, the first time we caught the same bus.

And not to mention, it is not lady-like to make the first move.

Of course, I've been to his bar where he drinks; I put that down to accidental or chance encounter.

If we are meant to be together, we will surely meet again, because like they say, "third time is a charm."

And that would be fate working; I would even go as far as to say cupids' arrow is at work.

Look at me; I am such a mess; I've never acted like this before; I mean, I've seen other girls doing it.

By doing it, I meant falling in love, not sex. I thought we clarify that.

I just thought I was different; well, anyway, I'm going to leave it in the hands of the Gods and fate.

Well, I still have his number in my back pocket of my jeans,

Oh shit, the jeans are in the wash,

OMG!

Well, I guess it is only in the hands of the higher power now.

I really should've rung him; what're the chances that we will meet or bump into each other a third time. I'm such a fool.

Well, this is what happened next:

22.01.2003

The Barbeque

I would meet my friend, so I asked my mother for a lift, but my mother was in a rush, so she dropped me in the area close by rather than drop me at my friend's house.

So, I was walking down the road listening to my music, and all of a sudden, the guy from the bus came out of a house that I was walking past.

He was carrying beer, and a lot of it, I might add. I mean, one part of me started smiling because it was fate intervening.

And the other part was appalled because each time I saw this guy, he was around alcohol.

So, he comes up to me, and he says "hi" and tells me that that is where he lives.

He invites me inside his house, and without giving it a second thought, I jumped at the chance to be in his company.

Because I wasn't going to risk for fate to intervene for the fourth time

We went inside and had a long discussion of everything and anything. I remember smiling as he introduced me to his mother. I was a little surprised, but I must admit I also felt at home. Perhaps it was just this guy and the way he was.

He seemed to be a free spirit; well, free until I cage him. Lol.

I remember he was talking about everything. But he wasn't talking about how we would end up together.

I mean, come on, you have a woman ready to have sex with you, and all you are doing is putting it off with idle and trivial discussions.

I can see his juicy, lovey lips move, but all I could hear the sound of his voice while he looked directly into my eyes.

Not even once did he look at my figure. Either he was a gentleman, or he was gay.

Just my luck, I meet the perfect guy, well, nearly perfect. And he's gay.

Or is he??

As he started to talk about his bedroom in the sense that he was proud of some accomplishment, of course, my mind was thinking that he was going to ask me out.

But the words 'bed' just made me excited.

"Oh, shit, I feel like a slag.

Well, I guess there's nothing wrong with being a slag from time to time.

Oh, I'm so horny.

I like it,"

These were my thoughts momentarily as he was yapping away.

So,
Anyway,

He said to me, "would you like to see my bedroom."

And without acknowledging what he had just asked me, the words left my lips saying, "yes, I'd love to date you."

I was waiting for him to ask me out. And for some reason, my mind was agreeing to a date. Instead, I had decided to go with him to his bedroom.

Being that I didn't want to embarrass myself further, we went to his bedroom upstairs.

It seemed that he didn't hear me say "yes to a date."

He seemed preoccupied in his weird world.

He started to show me his bedroom; it was a unique bedroom; it had some fascinating wallpaper with art that resembled an inside of the swimming pool.

He started to put some music on, not the kind of music you would think to put on for a man and woman. I mean, maybe romantic jazz music or something like that.

Instead, he put on some party music, and it was deafening; I asked him to turn the music down.

Which he did,

Soon as he put the music down, he uttered the words.

"So, do you see us dating?"

He caught me off guard, and I uttered the only words that I could think about at the time, which was, "let start as friends."

Then I said to him I have to go now, write down my phone number on a piece of paper, and give it to him.

He said to me, where do you think you're going; you're not going anywhere.

I realized that I was in his bedroom; I just thought the worst; I thought he would take advantage of me.

I just criticized myself in my head, stating, "well-done girl."

I had made it so easy for him; I just wanted to leave.

But at the same time, I felt safe; for some odd reason, it was just something about him.

I mean, if any other guy had said those words to me. I would've already kicked him in the crotch and made a run for the door.

But something inside me didn't want to leave; I don't know maybe I liked him that much, that I was risking my virginity this far.

He closed the bedroom door, and at this point, I knew that I might leave his bedroom without my virginity.

I didn't want to struggle, so I was just forced to smile and close my eyes as he came close.

After a minute or so, I open my eyes, and he was on one knee with a rose in his hand, he reiterated.

"you're not going anywhere."

adding the words

"without a rose to mark the beginning of our friendship."

That day I knew I had met somebody that was going to be my man.

I threw myself at the man, giving him every opportunity to take me.

And yet, he was nothing but a gentleman.

So, I left that day with my virginity intact.

But I kept having these incessant thoughts that if he had just touched me at least once, I could have fantasized about something.

The thought got worse from here on in.

I guess I just needed to get laid.

Sometimes even some of us women need some lovely laying and head-boarding.

Again, these are the thoughts that frequently came into my mind.

I mean, come on, I didn't even get a hug; I saw his 18-inch biceps, and I just wanted him to rough me up a little bit.

Or, at the very least, hold me.

But one thing is for sure; I was going to take him; he was going to be my man.

Because there is nothing sexier in a man that talks to you and not your breasts.

I knew it that day; I was going to give my virginity up to this guy.

But,

I couldn't believe it; I was considering being with him, a person that drunk alcohol.

It's not like I was marrying him.

Perhaps it was just dating for a while,

So anyway!

As it stood, it seemed like I was following him around,

Because I met him on his way home the first time on the bus, and then went to the bar he drank in. and then walked past his house.

It was indeed a weird time, not to mention the timing, because I was just about to go to university, and he had newly opened a new business.

So, I couldn't see a future, but I could see us having some fun.

Oh, I want him all over me, I'm just going to say it, I want him to rub Jell-O all over me and lick it off.

I'm so dirty,

I feel so dirty,

But it feels so good.

Oh, I need help!

So, this is what happened next!

The friendship starts

I said, "let's be friends,"

I wanted to say forget about friends, let's get it together.

Don't get me wrong, but I'm a 19 old virgin who wants to experience a man's embrace with all his thrust.

I sometimes wonder what it would be like with him taking charge of me and caressing my breasts and playing in my lady garden.

After all, I have seen this first-hand.

I remember when I was 15 years old. My father's friend came to stay with us. And every night we all would sit in front of the TV to watch films.

My father's friend would ask me to sit beside him. And then place a blanket over us to keep warm. It was so cozy and comfortable if he hadn't tried to squeeze my breasts and tried to put his hands in my pants.

The funny thing is I told my mother. And they did nothing about it. Because it would be embarrassing for the family, so, for the duration of his stay, his hands would be on my breasts and fanny.

Luckily it was only a very short stay.

So, this is why I wanted to be with somebody I chose before I was forced to be with somebody that I didn't want to be with.

Sometimes families think they know best.

Anyway,

I hope this friendship is short-lived because I do want to have a boyfriend. I come from a post-modern family whereby their views on boyfriends are of old ways.

So, I have nobody that would understand me having a boyfriend.

And of course, there is that; I am looked upon as the most responsible out of my siblings.

You could say I am the geek of the family.

Sometimes I get irate because my siblings don't realize that I have a pussy too.

And sometimes, I like to touch myself to experience what it must be like when a man does it to me.

Sometimes I like to pinch my pom-pom and caress my dishes.

But at the same time, I don't want to be with a pervert; I want to be with somebody to help me explore my body in detail.

I don't want to be with somebody like my dad's friend. He never looked me in the eyes. He just helped himself.

And also,

I remember my dad's friend getting hard for less than a song would last. Which is pathetic; I didn't know whether to feel disgusted or feel like I was too much for him to handle.

They say even from bad experiences; we tend to learn lessons of life.

I remember one thing above all that my man was never going to come less than a song.

No point just jumping aboard for less than a song. Is it?

I need something more than wham bam thanks; you are mam.

I sit here most days daydreaming about the way my man will hold me gently and put his hands around my neck, then put his fingers through my hair, as our lips touch for the very first time. I want him to slide his hands down my back until he gets to my waist and then hold me tight until we climax.

I want to be kissed passionately; I like the kiss to be so phenomenal that I come before his lips leave mine.

I'm waiting by the phone nearly every day, almost every hour, almost every minute.

I know about the three-day rule.

I don't know why we have it.

And of course, we are friends,

So, why isn't he calling?

30.01.2003

Ring,

ring,

ring,

finally,

finally, the phone rings

It is him!

Instead of hello, he said.

"I don't want to be friends with you."

My heart just started beating fast.

He followed shortly with, "I can't stop thinking about you, and I'm having that kind of thoughts that a boyfriend would have of a girlfriend," he said.

I could hear the slur on his voice, he wasn't sober, but I carried on listening to what he had to say.

Tbh (to be honest), if he had been anybody else, I would've already have put the phone down.

But he was inside my head, and each time he communicated with me, I was surprised how he would come across.

I mean, it was like he was trying to be a gangster and a nice guy at the same time.

He was tickling my fancy, through the realization of being with a bad boy who seems to act gently.

I mean, imagine someone that could handle themselves and then look after you too.

At the same time, put you on a pedestal.

He came out with, "I'll be any man you want me to be."

I mean, I was shocked and surprised at the same time.

Because I'm thinking, hey girl, you found the prince that you can control.

I remember the further said, "it was my way or no way."

And he followed with that he was happy to take things slow.

But my voice was like. What do you mean slow? You idiot.

I'm ready for you to take me from all sides.

But my answer was I feel the same.

I mean, come on! I wasn't going to put it out over the phone.

So, we decided that we were going to be more than friends.

I must say, I never would agree to something like this. It was too straightforward.

"I mean, we haven't even dated yet." Is what I should've said.

But he has this way of getting me to trust him. It was like he asked the question, confident of the answer.

Then agree to the question himself.

And expected me to follow along. I mean, he said something like.

If I were with you, then I would give up all my friends because I would not need anyone else in my life; it was my frame of mind at that time.

Of course, that's right.

The thing with the answer to that question, I have only one solution.

Let me explain; if I disagree, then I'm potentially giving him time to spend with his friends.

And that's never good, especially when you're trying to control somebody.

The first role in controlling anybody you have to what I call "singledom."

It is only my way if he doesn't seek advice from somewhere else.

But soon as I agree with him, I am also partially agreeing that we should be together.

So, in effect, he has pushed me towards being with him.

So, my mind starts to think, is this happening to me.

Because he has iterated through the last question.

It causes deep concern; I mean, is he intelligent and trying to control me.

By making me think that I might be able to control him

I wanted a man that I could control.

What I find getting my way

I always like being tricked into bed.

See, it's easy for guys; they get up the next day and have a shower.

It's not that simple; we have to wait until the end of the month to spring clean the lady in between.

So, I must be careful about how I am giving myself to this guy.

I agreed to go out with him, but I had to set specific terms. I told him until I got to know him better, he wasn't allowed to touch me.

I told him I would not even kiss him.

Do you know what he said to me?

"Every woman dreams of that perfect moment."

And then

"That moment when they are embracing a new man for the first time."

Followed by,

"And it is that moment that defines the entire relationship."
Lastly, he said,

"So, for a man, the pressure is insatiable. So, I am going to back off and let you decide when that moment is going to happen for us."

I mean, come on!

I walked right into that one!

It's like whatever I say to him. Life seems to become more comfortable for him.

He passes the decision over to me.

I mean, talk about pressure.

I haven't even been kissed. How am I going to pick up that moment?

Well, I guess.

There won't be any surprises.

I couldn't figure this guy out. No matter what I said to him.

He seems to agree. And give me even more than I asked for.

I also told him that I didn't believe in sex before marriage.

I mean, I can't wait for him to hold me and ravish me.

Because I want him to be my first

But I wasn't going to make it easier for him.

After all, I was 99% sure.

I guess when you see something that you want. You can't stop yourself until you get what you desire.

So, he said to me, "we should go out next week."

Followed by me can't wait to see you.

I had to whisper at this point because my family had come home after dinner.

Because we were still phone buddies at this point

He found my whispering voice smooth and sexy.

He asked me, "why are you whispering." I told him that I couldn't talk just now.

He said, okay, I will see you next week to go out for a casual predating chat.

I said, 'predating chat?'

He said I want to take you up properly, but we need to get to know one another as you said.

So, we can connect, and then we can start to build the perfect moment for you to kiss me.

For a moment there, I was gasping for air because I wanted to see his cheeky grin; I bet he was laughing his arse off.

But I was blushing and at the same time finding myself lip-licking myself.

The more we talk, the more I knew I wanted him.

I knew I wanted to sleep with him.

He was just so lovely, in a gangster bad / boy gentleman type of person.

So, I agreed to meet him for a predating chat.

He said,

Before he put the phone down, "If you feel you want to talk to me any time before, then please feel free to call me." Because I don't want to seem needy and bombard you with text or phone calls, so, I will leave the ball in your court.

I wanted to say your cheeky little beeswax. "Please, leaving the ball in my court, indeed," "the ball is always in my side of the court."

And, then I wanted to say,

"That's nice, see you next week, my sweet darling sexy 'nice ass man.'"

I mean, he did have a lovely ass.

But really, I left it at:

"ahh, that's nice."

As you do

After all, he wanted to get in my knickers, so why make it easy for him?

Haha.

Later on:

I spoke to my friend, Kiki, over the phone.

I told her that "I was going out with this guy."

And she was like, "tell me it's not the guy from the bus."

I was like, "well, it's the guy from the bus, the bar, and I walked past his house."

"And went into his bedroom." Wink, nudge wink nudge 😉😉😉

My friend went ballistic.

She said,

"what the hell."

Followed with,

"What were you thinking?"

After a 10-minute lecture, she calms down.

And I told her that I think he is the one.

Suddenly, there was a further 10 minutes of niceness as my friend changed her tone of voice.

She said, "I knew you liked him."

I said, "yeah, but I'm scared,"

My friend said, "of what."

I said, "of being hurt."

She said it's not like you're going to drop your knickers for him.

Because Kiki wanted to only sleep with her husband after her marriage, she was very narrow-minded that way.

And she thought I was the same, little did she know. I was ready to drop my knickers the moment I laid eyes on him—Lmao (laughing my ass off).

So, it was difficult to tell her that I was masturbating three times a week.

Can you imagine if I had said that to her?

Haha,

That would've been the end of our friendship.

So, after a while, still on the phone. I said it would be alright if I kissed him.

Kiki said, "what, what, whatever do you mean."

I quickly change the words,

I mean, "if he kisses me." Of course,

I didn't want to tell her of the blunder that I have just made.

Kiki said, "use your lips and close your eyes. If it goes on too long, stick your tongue in his mouth."

I said, "what do you mean, that's dirty!"

Kiki said, "somebody told me, this is what common folk or French kissing is like. It's when each other's tongues are in each other's mouth."

I was like, "what, and at the same time getting wet down below. I mean, I was intrigued. But I didn't know how to French kiss him."

I said, "Kiki, can I practice on you? She said, "have you been drinking."

Haha,

Followed with, "have you lost your mind."

I said, "you know I don't drink alcohol, Kiki." "stop being horrible; you know that I don't know how to do this properly."

Kiki said in a firm but friendly voice, "look, Didi, I don't mind kissing you. But I don't want both of our first experiences of the special moment with one another.

And Kiki followed with,

"I tell you what, Didi, go out with your boyfriend. Kiss him. And I'll do the same. Then we will meet back and kiss. To check everything is okay. What do you think?

Silence

Long pause,

I said, in an agitated state, "really, so let me get this right I'm going to kiss my boyfriend, and then you're going to kiss him too. And then we kiss. I'm not too sure about this.

Kiki said, "are you out of your mind seriously? Have you been drinking?"

Followed with,

"I merely meant you kiss your guy, and I kiss my guy, and before you get this confused too. We are going to be on different dates, in separate places."

I said, "I see."

Followed by

Kiki, I don't know what to say. I'm just scared; I might want to try other things with you too.

Kiki said,
"Listen, Didi, let's take one step at a time."

"Sometimes, these things have a way of working out for themselves."

"Kiki, thanks so much, is what I should've said."

Instead,

I said, "Kiki, should I kiss you the week after then!"

The phone went dead.

Perhaps her credit ran out.

07.02.2003

The pre-date!

I went to meet him at this high-end lavish bar that he had booked. I've got you thinking; I don't drink. So, why is it taking me to a bar?

However, my rational thinking was left at home. I was going to go with the flow.

As I arrived at the bar, he was waiting outside for me as my taxi pulled up. He went towards the car and opened the door. And paid for the cab; he also put his hand out for me to hold him as I got out.

So, I'm thinking of an excellent start. I mean, it was like chivalry or something like that. I dunno!

So, we went into the bar, and I noticed it wasn't quiet and was crowded somewhat too, But it seemed there was a separate section of this bar towards the rear of the building. Where it was a bit quieter; of course, a lot more Romantic. A place where I imagine guys take women to get into their knickers faster.

After all, I wasn't ready to drop my knickers just yet. A woman needs wining and dining before all that.

Straightaway, as we walked through the door, he said, "today is a pre-date, I realize that. But it is a Friday night. And this is the quietest place that I could find. Because I don't want to hear anything but your voice."

I mean, I'm not a blabbermouth, but it's nice to know that he will listen to me. So many men out there. Who seems to blabber all night long about anything I'm nothing? I must say that it was refreshing for a guy to talk this way.

As we went and sat down at our table. The chair seems like it hovered out of the way. He was very intuitive but relaxed. It's like he did things without thinking. He wasn't trying to act the part of a gentleman. This guy was a gentleman.

I wanted to say something wrong about him. Or at least something to make him seem less perfect. But I was at a loss. The more I looked for his imperfections. I found generosity, humbleness, and a sense of kindness.

I must say, I did try to trick him because I wore these tight trousers and a part revealing top. I also uplifted the girls. Not something I usually do. But I wanted to see if he was looking at me. Or was he in it for the features?

He gazed into my eyes and never looked away for a second since the minute I arrived. Why do you talk to me? He was very brief, and to the point? But when I was short and to the end. He wanted me to elaborate. When do I ask him to elaborate too? He said, "I'm a listener, not a talker."

I was like, oh my God, I have landed on my feet here.

I smiled, and the waiter came over and poured the champagne. Before I could stop the waiter, I had a glass full of champagne. This was it; I was outraged. The imperfection that I was looking for. I had found it.

Boy, was he going to get it?

Shame he was such a nice guy too.

I said, "what do you think you are doing?" as I stood up slowly.

He immediately stood up straight. And called the waiter. He asked the waiter to show me the champagne bottle that he had just poured into my glass.

Although the bottle stated champagne, it was alcohol-free. It was like a fruit punch.

Boy, did I feel stupid? I wanted to run out of there.

But all of a sudden. He apologized to me. He said, "not your fault; the bouquet should've been tested before poured.

He went to the waiter and gave him the third degree. It was my fault. He had made such a fuss that nobody remembered what I said as everybody was focused on him.

That's when I realized, to save me embarrassment. He caused a scene for me to save face.

Then he quickly asked me if we were going to leave. Of course, I want you to run out the door as soon as possible. So, I said yes, and we swiftly left.

As we walked to another place that he knew of. Because funny enough, he had a backup place to go to. He said, just in case something went wrong, I plan for the worst.

But I stopped him in his tracks. And I told him. I don't put up with liars and cheaters. I'm going to ask you a question. And the answer that you give me has to be the truth.

He said, "I never lie, so please ask away."

I was like 'never lie,' what's the rolling my eyes, I'm thinking yeah sure whatever.

So, I asked him, did you, or did you not blame the waiter for something that was my fault.

He asked me before I answer. Would you like the truth? Or the truth. Because you can only have one

I mean, I was boggled because people don't ask you this kind of question. I mean, I don't know what you say. So, I just said, "just tell me the truth."

He said that your final answer.

He immediately looked into my eyes and said, "I will always back you up in public and correct you in private should that be necessary."

I was gobsmacked!

I mean, I want to kiss him right there and then.

Well, I did learn a bit.

Perhaps not far enough, because he moved forward and put his hands on my waist. I was expecting the French business in my mouth. But he gently pulled me towards him and embraced me with his bulging arms. And whispered gently into my ear, you will always be a priority in my life.

I got one of the best hugs that I've ever had. I didn't want to let go. I want to hold you all night. My hands were on his waist, and one of my hands found its way to his bum. "by mistake."

That night we walked, and we talked; I didn't feel like going to another place. So, we ended up at this takeaway eating out. It was funny because it seemed like I wasn't out with a guy. It looks like I was out with Kiki. You make me feel so comforted. And I told him so many things about myself. And he just listened. I mean, I must've been riveting on for some time. But each time I look at him. He smiled instinctively and intuitively.

Do you know how many men pretend to listen but really, they are just thinking about the fastest way to get into your knickers? Well, this one wasn't one of them. But I must admit I didn't want you to get into my knickers. But I was going to make him wait.

I told him I wasn't a one-night girl. I told him I was proper. He took a deep breath. And then took three steps forward; Then he pulled out his hand. And said, come on as my hand touched his hand, he said I'm here for the long haul. Take your time. I'm in no rush. I'm just glad we met in this crazy world.

I mean, what more can I say. I was ready to go up the aisle with him at that point.

As he walked me to my taxi, we passed a jazz musician playing a lovely song. He made me twirl, and at the same time, you drop some money into the guy's saxophone case. That's when I knew this guy was a moment pleaser.

I mean, come on, a woman has to work the guy out. I mean, that's what we do.

As I got into my taxi, I realize that he wasn't going to get in with me. I wanted to talk to have some more.

As the taxi took off, I saw him briefly run towards the cab, and then my phone rang.

He said I forgot to ask you out for Valentine's Day. Will you be my valentine on our actual date next week?

I was so full of emotion, on the words, yes, yeah, yes, left my lips. I guess that's what happens when you leave your thinking hat at home.

I went home that night with a smile on my face, which lasted right up to the next time we communicated.

I'm not much for fairy tales, but it seemed that I had jumped slap bang into the middle of the one.

Knight in shining armor, well, I guess we can't have it all. But he was shining, and he did act like a night because he knew that act of chivalry.

As he opens the door each time, I was going to enter. I mean, he even gave me his jacket when we were walking. I can see him feeling cold, but he just smiled. He had a lovely smile and a magnificent bum. I just wanted to lick his ass, literally.

He also texted me to make sure that I got home safely, or was he checking up that I went straight home! Only time will tell, I suppose!

14.02.2003

Valentine's day and the 1st date

He asked me to meet him at this bar, I mean of all the places in the world. He had to pick a bar. I must admit I was a bit dubious, but I was also intrigued. He wasn't like the guys that I had seen before, even though he was drunk. I felt connected to him, I dunno!

I guess we'll have a known who she wants to give up her virginity to. I guess you just do it. I mean, a woman commonly knows within the first five seconds whether she wants to sleep with a guy or not. And for some odd reason, I had these kinds of urges for this guy.

I remember I got there before him. And he arrived moment after all dressed up like he was going to a prom. And here was me wearing my casual outfit, so we met, and he started talking about his day. But I just glared at him. I don't know why. I just wanted him to hold me. After all, I had heard all the stories about people dating and having sex. I wish to experience something. I guess I was gagging for it. But I wasn't going to make it easy for him.

We went inside, and after a few moments of him talking incessantly. He finally put his hand on my leg as his touch came closer to my girlfriend downstairs. Something weird happened to me. It was like a discharge or something. I tried to hold it in, but the closer he got, the harder he got. I remember him moving closer and nibbling on my ear. I bit my lip as his breath touched and tickled my neck. I remember the hair on the back of my neck stand up. Right then and there, I would have let him feel me. I wanted to put my tongue in his mouth for some reason.

I was all wet and nowhere to come. He was coming on slowly. And I need you to come. So, I sat at the table listening to his Twaddle. Until his words took control of my emotions, and his touch became unbearably lucid. All of a sudden, I just grabbed him. I needed to hold him because what was wet inside had now come outside.

Luckily for my granny panties, which I was wearing because I was close to that time of the month. I immediately asked to go to the lady's room.

Because I needed to clear away the mess I had made, I had to sit on the toilet seat when I got to the lady's room. At the same time, I pulled my jeans down. I had come right through, my granny panties. I was so embarrassed. Because I hadn't come like that before, and as it seemed, I couldn't wear those panties. So, I took them off and wiped my little girlfriend as I pull my jeans up. I could feel I wisp of hair around my girlfriend down below. I mean, this was the first time I was going anywhere without my knickers. I must say each step I took; I became aroused. I have never known such freedom from such restrictions that we pose on ourselves. I remember I couldn't stop smiling. After all, if my girlfriend was happy, then I was delighted. So, both of us, both contempt and satisfied, left the lady's room.

I remember walking back to the table giggling and smiling. And him looking at me like he hadn't seen a woman before. I knew something was going to happen. But I hadn't shaved my legs.

He started talking again, and I remember thinking, 'when is it going to touch me again.' I mean, he could speak; boy, this guy was going on and on and on. I needed something. So, I looked around the room and realized many women were showing off their lady parts. So, I unzipped my jacket in the hope that he would caress my breasts. Don't get me wrong; I just wanted a man's touch. I want to know the difference between my touching and his touching. I mean, when I'm having a bath, I sometimes play with myself because I just want to know what it feels like when a man does it. I can't wait until he throws me all over that bed. I better come down; I don't want to make it too easy for him. But he needs to grow a pair.

As the date went on, he asked if I wanted to go to the cinema. I am immediately thought of a dark and secluded environment. Where he could founder me to his heart desire. And where I could hold his sausage. I hope it is a reasonable size because my friend said, "sometimes size matters." She also said, "largest is pain, shortest is counting time, and a medium-size tickles the walls."

I stood there biting my lip and looking downwards at his hotdog of a sausage. I just kept thinking about what my friend said, and I just kept wondering. He then asked me again if that a 'yes.' I find myself spaced out, so I said yes to me holding his manhood. And he thought I said yes to going to the cinema. So, when he said, come on, then let's do it. For a moment there, I just froze. My mind was like, put my clothes off and do me here and now. Of course, this is perfect gentleman put his hands around my waist and guided me towards the exit.

As we walked, I could feel another discharge coming. I couldn't believe it. I mean multiple discharges in my pants; I was feeling wet and horney by this stage. So, I just focused on his voice and what he was saying. Of course, he was just trying to impress me by making me believe he was some sort of businessman, but I could see he was nothing more than a student. A student who seems to have a giant sausage, all the way to the cinema, I just kept biting my lip. I want to do him so much. I wanted him to ride me like a man on a bull.

We arrived at the cinema, and he bought the tickets with the popcorn, hot dogs and drinks. He asked do you need anything more before the film starts; I said no; in my mind, I said, I want to nibble on your hotdog, and then you can ravish me. We walk inside the cinema hall. And we sat down. The film started as the lights dimmed down. I noticed his left arm hugging me as his right hand was gently grazing my right leg. He moved in close as I breathed in. He asked me to kill him if anything interesting happened in the film. As I looked away, he unzipped my jeans. I didn't feel all that different because I had no knickers on. But when he stroked me. I nearly jumped out of my seat. But he was holding me in such a way that I didn't move much.

He started to touch me. I looked at him and asked him to stop. But, in my mind, I was like 'finally.' So yes, in this case, 'no' means 'yes.'

He whispered into my ear, "I am going to finger you." Call me naïve, but I didn't know at the time what fingering was. Because I didn't want to be marked as stupid, I just said, "okay, that's fine then."

I remember him breathing on my neck, and then all of a sudden, I felt this intense urge to hold him. It was like he was touching me right there. In my mind, I was screaming, I was like, oh yes, oh yes. He started pushing it in deeper. I felt a bit uncomfortable, but I didn't want him to stop. I just wanted him to keep rubbing me slowly and gently. At the time, I didn't realize, but he was having finger sex with me. It was so intense for me. I was on top of the moon. I could only imagine what his sausage was going through. I just wanted to grab it, but I didn't want it to seem effortless.

It was finally happening, but I wanted a little bit more. He started to caress my breasts and pull my top up as he slid his hand, effortlessly underneath my cleavage. It was like he knew exactly what I wanted. Suppose he asked me to go to the bathroom with him at that precise moment. The answer would've been yes, yes, oh bloody yes. Luckily for us, there were not many people in the cinema hall. So, we just got carried away.

I mean, we didn't even realize when the film stopped. I remember he put his jacket on the floor and asked me to lay on it. He said he just wanted a bit more space. We got onto the floor. And he pulled my Jeans down effortlessly. I'm going to start playing with me. I was a bit concerned because we hadn't even had our first kiss. It was like he had bypassed the first base and jump to the second and third base. So, I asked him to stop.

He said, "okay, I'll just finish off."

I said, "don't put it inside me,"

He said, "it's not like that, I'm just finishing off,"

I was a bit confused, but I could see his pants still on. So that gave me some comfort. But I was still confused about what he was finishing off to.

Again, I didn't want to sound stupid, so I just agreed and said, "okay, sure."

He asked me to lay back while he put his head between my legs. I tried to hold his head. Because I didn't know what he was doing, all of a sudden, I felt his tongue on my girlfriend. I mean, I felt aroused and disgusted at the same time. He was putting his tongue inside my girlfriend down below. I mean, it felt good, but it also had a unique aroma. So, I couldn't imagine anybody willingly tasting it.

But he seemed to enjoy it. Even though I had never shaved my lady garden ever, how did you find it so fast with his tongue? I mean, sometimes I would have to use a comb to take a wee.

He kept making these noises like somebody eating a pizza. At that time, I thought perhaps what it would feel like if I put his sausage in my mouth. I suppose I could give it a go, as I thought out openly in my mind. But that is the only thought that I had. My mind has stopped drinking since my little girlfriend seems to be indulging continuously.

All of a sudden, something unexpected happened. I came like never before. But it was like I was taking a wee. I mean, I must've pissed on his face. He managed to move out of the way, but I did get him, I'm sure of it. I felt so embarrassed. Yet he was filled with happiness; he said, "you must be a squirter." I didn't want to answer.

But I had to ask what is squirter was. So, I just said 'squirter,' whatever do you mean.

He said, "it's when you come, and you can't hold it in. Very few women can do this. And I'm glad that you can do it with me."

I was shocked and surprised at the same time, not to mention satisfied. So, I pulled up my jeans. And he stopped me. He said, "as they are down, may I see your bum."

I was already exposed, but because I was satisfied, I said, "I would come around and put my Jeans up, and you can have a look."

He said, "I would rather you just bend over and let me take a look."

He followed with, "I won't belong. I just want to take a peek."

I was embarrassed at the time, but I did agree to do this.

I turned around and bent over with my bum exposed.

He immediately held my bum and kissed both sides of my bum cheeks. And then put his tongue in between my river line.

I smile intently because all I could think about was the phrase, "talk about someone licking the bosses' arse," haha.

I pulled my jeans. And walk towards the exit for a while, tucking in my top. I mean, I was wet front and back. I need to go to the lady's restroom straightaway. "I remember shouting, I'll meet you at the exit, as I whisked out the door.

I wasn't in the restroom for too long because I didn't want you to go away thinking about something else. I liked this person in my life.

Was he the one? I don't know? But I want to learn more. So, I took I look at myself in the mirror and said to myself, "I've got this,"

He asked if I was hungry as I came out of the restroom.

I remember thinking, 'yes' I would like your sausage.

He said, "I'm afraid I've eaten my sausage, but I can get you another, hotdog."

I quickly rolled my eyes and kept my head down because I realized I had just said that out loud.

He went to get me a hotdog, and I medially said I feel like some chicken.

And I wish that that time he didn't click on to thinking I meant his manhood,

So, we went and had something to eat, and it was the quietest he had been. After all, he had seen me. But at the same time, I was a bit embarrassed because I hadn't shaved. And he must've at least seen my thighs. And noticed my overgrown lady garden.

So, we just had some food at this magnificent diner. The food was terrific. And every bite was better than the last. So, I enjoy the food; I mean, at times, I did think that I was enjoying his manhood. But I don't know, that day as I looked at him eating both me and his food. I realized that he was someone that I wanted to get to know. Well, more so than we had already done. After all, I still needed to have a look at what's under his hood. There was laughter in my head. But only a sneaky smile on my face as I finished off my food.

He later asked me if I wanted to take a walk, from which I gathered, he was a bit nervous. Because he was talking erratically and hysterically about anything and everything that came to his mind, I could see him struggling with his nervous laughter and idle conversations. So, I just held his hand as I leaned into him and said, "just told me."

As we walked embracing each other, he said would you like to go for a drink. I could see that he hadn't had a drink all day. So, we went into a bar to have a drink. He tried to kiss me in the bar, and I didn't like him. He was a bit surprised, and I was wondering why I pushed him away. So, we sat there, and he said, "it is Valentine's Day. We should kiss."

It wasn't that I didn't want to kiss him. It was that I didn't know how to kiss him. So, I was glad he brought me to a bar full of people who were kissing each other. So, as he started talking, I guess I started observing the people around me and how they were maneuvering their lips over one another. I didn't want to make it obvious, but I needed to know because I needed to make sure that there was some kiss by the end of this night. Well before 00.00 hours. When, of course, the next day would begin.

He was handling me by now. But I didn't want to be handled in public.

So, I asked him if we could go somewhere else.

He agreed, and we left.

We strolled down the road hand-in-hand. And we found this lovely little place that seems to be quiet. So, we went inside and had a drink. We sat down in a dark, secluded area. He took a sip of his drink and put it down. He came close to me and said, "you look beautiful tonight."

He leaned in, brushing my hair away. I think he was going to kiss me, so looking at the people in the other bar. I just open my mouth and stick my tongue in his. And we started doing something with our lips.

We were moving side to side and drooling all over each other. Our tongues were playing water sports. And at that moment, I just realized that I had from my man. I just felt so safe in his embrace. I had never closed my eyes and opened myself to a man before. We kissed most of the night, and I think towards the end of the night. I became somewhat of an expert by the end of the night.

It was an exciting night. I had been fingered, caressed, and felt up on the same night. I'm not to mention I had my first snog after the man licked my arse.

Something to put in my diary, I suppose!

It was a memorable night, one that I will cherish for a long while to come. And I hope there's many more comes, if you catch my drift.
I want to tell you some more of the secrets of what happened next.

So, follow us in book 2, called Divina. By Indy Cruz.

Printed in Great Britain
by Amazon